To Bernice MacFadden,
the woman who taught me about
horses and people...with love

Patricia Lee Gauch, Editor
Book design by Donna Mark. Text set in Galliard.

Houghton Mifflin Edition, 2001

Printed in the U. S. A.

ISBN: 0-618-06250-5

3456789-B-06 05 04 03 02 01

Mrs. Mack

Patricia Polacco

HOUGHTON MIFFLIN BOSTON • MORRIS PLAINS, NJ

California • Colorado • Georgia • Illinois • New Jersey • Texas

DOGPATCH

It was the summer of my tenth year. I was spending it with my dad, in Michigan, just as I had since I was four. My brother, Richie, my dad, and I were sitting on the talk porch, gnawing on sweet corn, and watching fireflies shimmer up from the newly mowed grass.

Dad grew unusually quiet, thoughtful, then leaned back against the porch step, loosened his belt, and sighed. "Yessir, I think this is going to be the summer, Patricia." I waited for the longest time for the next word, searching his face for a clue. "This is the summer that you are going to learn to ride."

My heart leapt in my chest because Dad knew my special dream—of having a horse of my very own. Learning to ride this summer meant only one thing—that he was going to get me a horse!

"When, Da?" I managed to squeal, and I turned cartwheels for the pure excitement of it.

He fell forward. "Tomorrow! How's that, my little filly? Tomorrow."

The next morning as Richie packed for summer camp, I put on the new riding clothes that Momma had gotten for me in San Francisco, "just in case." After all, this was the day that I was going to get my own horse. After we dropped Richie off for the bus to camp, Dad headed down the highway toward Lansing. "A college town," my mother always called it because a university was there.

"Where we going, Da?" I asked, barely able to contain my excitement. Maybe the stable would be somewhere near the college.

"You'll see," he sang out as he drove along.

I tried to imagine just what the horse would look like. I wondered if it would be anything like the one that I always dreamed of. Maybe I'd never have to go to those dumb old pony ride places, where the pony was led around in a circle by a huge metal wheel like a tired merry-go-round. That wasn't real riding!

When we got to Lansing, Dad drove by the college, past the city center and Potters Park. When he finally started to slow, I looked out the window. The houses were run down, some of them were even shacks. I realized that we were in Dogpatch! The roughest part of town.

Dad had made a terrible mistake. There couldn't be any horses here!

Then we stopped. In front of the most shabby stable that I had ever seen. A horse trailer right next to a shack had a sign on it that said "Office." A couple of real tough-looking kids leaned against a hitching rail beside two tired-looking horses.

I could feel the tears well up in my eyes. Dad wasn't going to "get" me a horse at all. I didn't want to get out of the car, but Dad took my hand, so I did.

6

THE WOMAN WITH SNAKESKIN BOOTS

WE STOOD THERE for a while. My eyes took everything in. What an awful place, I thought. It was dirty and unfriendly, and there was a real mean-looking old man leaning over the fence next door. He spat on the ground and mumbled something.

"You kids seen Mrs. Mack?" my father finally asked one of the tough kids.

Just as they were about to answer, an old 1952 Impala rattled up in front and sputtered to a stop. I had never seen so much dust on a car in my life. The only clear spots on the windshield were where the wipers had made a pass across it.

I leaned over and looked inside. I saw a woman with high cheekbones and a broad smile with one overlapping front tooth, just like mine. She had glistening blue eyes and tousled brown hair that fell to her shoulders. I felt her eyes drink me in. We breathed together for a moment.

"Hey, shugah, you must be Pat!" She had such a deep southern accent that she made it sound like "Pate," not "Pat."

"Patricia," my dad announced, "This is Mrs. Mack. She's forgotten more about horses than most people will ever know in a lifetime," he said with genuine admiration.

The woman—she had on snakeskin boots!—got out of the car and walked me over to the two kids.

"Pat, meet Donnie and Nancy," she said. Their eyes looked me up and down. "Show Pat around," Mrs. Mack said as she pushed me toward them.

"That's one fancy outfit....Where you from anyway, Hollywood?" the boy said as we walked to the back stalls. I could feel my face flush. He nudged the girl; they both laughed.

I didn't belong here! Why had my dad brought me here? I didn't like these kids at all, and they sure didn't like me. And there was that old man. He was watching us again. He didn't look any friendlier than he did before.

We walked from stall to stall. Nancy and Donnie told me the names of the

horses—Salty, Buster, Lady, Pal—but I could hardly remember anything they were saying because I felt so out of place.

Then Nancy jumped up on the fence rail. I climbed up, too. "That one there is Apache!" she said, pointing to a horse out in the corral. "A strawberry Appaloosa, Mrs. Mack's horse. Almost nobody rides him besides her."

"Only one other horse in this here stable that is as good as Apache," Donnie said, pointing to the back holding pen.

"No one rides her, though," Nancy said.

I squinted into the pen. There, standing in the broken sunlight, was the most beautiful animal I had ever seen in my life.

"This here one is Penny," Nancy said, none too friendly about it.

"Ain't she grand!" Donnie said as if he'd forgotten I was there.

But he was right. My eyes followed her contours. She was perfect. A beautiful buckskin mare with black socks. Her closely cropped mane rode up her arched neck to a full top crop. Her tail was short, but she held it as if it had been "set" up for a fancy horse show. She stood there almost motionless. As the sun danced through the leaves of the overhanging tree, her coat shone like a bright copper penny.

The horse took a step, her muscles danced through her legs. She looked right at me with her beautiful intelligent eyes, her ears cupped forward as she made a whuffling sound that rippled through her nostrils.

This is the one! I thought. She was everything that was beautiful about a horse. She was my dream. Suddenly, it didn't matter that I was in Dogpatch, or that these kids didn't like me. Nothing mattered to me anymore except having the chance to be there with Penny.

For the rest of that first day I just stood and watched the bustle that went on around me. Donnie and Nancy ignored me—they took renters on trail rides. Whenever they returned, they went into the office to have coffee. I felt useless. I started to feel lonely, especially when Mrs. Mack left to pick up new bridles. I found myself going back to where Penny was and standing and looking at her and dreaming of a time that I might be good enough to ride her.

WHEN DAD CAME to pick me up after work, I didn't say much. But the next morning I was up bright and early, ready to go. I wore my jeans and a tee shirt this time. No ribbons or rhinestones.

"Hey, Hollywood!" I heard Donnie call out as we arrived. "You look like one of us today!" He smiled, and I smiled back.

But Nancy bolted over between us. "She'll never be one of us...too soft." Then she handed me a pitchfork. "Here, clean out the manure in number three, six, and eight stalls. When you're through with those, curry down Pal and Butch. Someone put them away last night without cooling them down and brushing them."

Where is Mrs. Mack? I wondered.

I shoveled, pitchforked, curried, swept, and cleaned. Sweat dripped down my chin. But I finished my chores before Nancy, and cleaned more stalls.

"Not bad for a city girl," she sneered.

Just then I felt a strong hand in the middle of my back. It was Mrs. Mack. "Nice job," she said. Then she looked at me. "Okay, shugah, let's get you started on a horse today!"

14

"Am I going to ride?" I stammered, feeling a little afraid.

"You sure are!" she answered.

"By myself?" I sputtered.

"All by yourself."

MEET PAL

PAL IS THE GENTLEST HORSE I have. I wouldn't put you on anything you weren't ready for, shugah," Mrs. Mack assured me the next day, as I stepped in her hand and threw my leg over Pal's back.

The saddle seemed hard and unbelievably small. The ground looked miles below me. "Keep your heels down"; "Sit back into the saddle"; "Ease the rein gently in the direction you want to go." Mrs. Mack kept talking to me.

Finally she led Pal across the road to the large corral. Every step Pal took seemed to rattle my bones.

The next thing I knew, Mrs. Mack opened the gate and let go of Pal's bridle, and I was alone. Donnie and Nancy came in, too. For the first time in my life, I was riding a horse alone. It wasn't attached to a turning wheel.

"Keep your hands soft, Pat," Mrs. Mack called out from the fence.

"And don't hang on to the saddle horn, Hollywood!" Donnie said, and grinned at Nancy. She trotted around me. They rode so well. I could feel my tears again.

Just then I heard Mrs. Mack's voice. "You look like you were born on the back of a horse, shugah."

I could feel the sun shining on my face. And I could almost feel my heartbeat keeping time with Pal's plodding steps. One day I would leave that corral and be good enough to ride out on a trail. I would.

Every day for a whole week, I rode good old Pal in the corral. By the end of that first week, I had learned how to put a bridle on him, saddle him, and even how to back him up!

But then, one day as I was riding Pal across the street, he lurched sideways. I lost my balance and fell off. I struggled to hang on to the reins, so Pal just dragged me along.

"It's okay, Hollywood," Donnie was saying to me as he took the reins from my clenched fist when Pal finally stopped. His voice was soft and soothing. "This has happened to all of us."

Even Nancy helped me off the ground. "One thing you gotta do is get back on that horse and ride him around the corral one more time, even if you can taste the fear," she said.

They both were smiling at me for the first time. I swallowed the fear, got back on, and rode Pal around the corral three more times.

Mrs. Mack was standing with Donnie and Nancy. A huge, round man came bustling across the street from the stable and stood next to her. He had messy red hair, a huge red mustache, red cheeks, and a crooked cigar wedged between his teeth. I found out later he was "Doc Beck, the best darn veterinarian in all Michigan."

As the days passed into weeks, I graduated from old Pal. I rode Buster, a stocky bay, and Taffy, a pretty buckskin. Mrs. Mack even let me go out on short trail rides with Donnie and Nancy on Salty. And one day she paired me up with Nancy and a paying customer to go out on a trail!

But at the end of every day, I always went into the holding pen where Penny was to kiss her good-bye. I'd climb into the stall with her, pull up an overturned bucket, and sit there with her. Sometimes she'd plunge her muzzle into the top of my head and muss up my hair.

Sometimes she'd whuffle, and sniff my ears with her nostrils. Most of the time, we'd just sit there together. I longed to ride her. It would be an answer to a nightly prayer.

One day as I arrived at the stables Mrs. Mack announced the next horse I'd ride would be Duke, normally Donnie's mount. Mrs. Mack thought I was good enough to try him.

First I rode him in the corral—we all did with a first mount. Mrs. Mack watched carefully. When she was sure I could handle him, she let me go out on the trail with Donnie and Nancy.

We were coming back from that ride, crossing a busy street near the stables, when a car came out of nowhere. Duke reared, the lurch of his neck wrenching the reins from my hands. He broke into a canter, then a dead run. I had lost control.

I was on a runaway horse, with no way to stop him!

Duke kept running faster and faster. I tried to reach down for the flailing reins, only to lose my balance and nearly fall off. Finally I got ahold of one of them. I pulled as hard as I could. This made Duke run in a circle. The circle got smaller and smaller, until he slowed down enough for me to reach the other rein and stop him.

When I got back, I put Duke away and went to Penny's pen. I climbed the fence next to her. She whuffled and came close to me. I put my arms around her. My tears rolled down her neck. Through my tears I could see a figure watching me from over the fence. It was the old man. I looked away. I didn't want him to see me crying. *Why not?*

I heard Mrs. Mack's voice say, "It's all right, Hap, I'm here with her now."

I looked up and she was talking to that old man! He turned and went toward his house. Then she hugged me.

"Every time I think I know horses, something happens!" I sobbed.

"Shugah," she said softly, "that's how you learn. The more of them you ride, the more experiences you have, the better rider you'll be."

"There is so much I don't know," I cried.

"Never feel you know it all. That's when you can get hurt."

"I'll never be the rider I want to be."

Mrs. Mack looked intently into my eyes. "Duke ran away with you, but you did exactly the right thing. You stayed with the saddle, you got ahold of one rein and pulled him into a circle! I never told you to do that. You're a natural, Pat, a natural."

Just then Penny came over to us and nudged my back with her head. Mrs. Mack looked surprised.

"How often do you come to this corral with Penny, Pat?" she asked.

"All the time I can," I answered.

"She doesn't take to people easily...." Her voice trailed off.

I heard a door slam. The man next door had gone inside.

"Do you know that old man, Mrs. Mack?" I asked.

"I can't say that I know him, but I know why he is the way he is."

"Seems like he watches me all the time when I work out," I said.

"He probably admires you, how hard you work to master riding. He, more than anyone, understands hours and hours of practice—he was a flyer with the Ringling Brothers circus. A trapeze artist."

22

That old man! "What happened to him?"

"One night during a performance he missed a 'catch' and dropped his brother. There was no net."

"Did he fall?"

"That's just it—he didn't. His brother did, and died from the fall. Hap blames himself. So now he's crippled up, see, crippled up inside, Pat."

The next morning when I came to the stables I brought a sack of molasses cookies that my grandma had made. I put them near Hap's back door and waited by the stable door until I saw him collect them and take them into his house.

From that day on, the cookies were as much a part of my mornings as visiting my sweet copper Penny. And one day when the blacksmith came to shoe her (Penny hated being shod so I stayed near to assure her), he pounded extra shoeing nails into rings for us kids. I asked him if he'd make a larger one for my dad. But instead of giving the ring to Dad, I put it in the next bag of cookies that I left at Hap's back door.

MY BEAUTIFUL COPPER PENNY

As each day passed and the summer was coming to an end, I yearned to ask Mrs. Mack if just once I could get on Penny's back. One rainy day I had almost summoned enough courage to approach her when Mrs. Mack asked me to go to the mill with her for feed.

We climbed into her Impala and set off. We didn't talk for a time. We just rode.

Then she said, "Have you ever wondered how you ended up here in Dogpatch with the rest of us?"

"My dad brought me here!" I answered.

"No, shugah, you ended up here because of a love that burns like a fire in your belly. Your love of horses! Your pa knew that I love them the same as you do, so he hooked us up." She smiled at me. "Not everybody has that kind of feeling for those animals, you know...." Her voice trailed off.

I knew exactly what she meant.

"They know, too, Pat....the horses. They know when they are around a pure soul that loves them. They can feel it in your hands. They can see it in your eyes. They can sense it in your heart."

I just looked at her. I wondered how she knew so much of my secret feelings.

"That's what brought you here. That's what brought Donnie and Nancy and all of the other kids who've come through my stables."

I smiled at her. I hadn't wanted to come to Dogpatch—ever—and I hadn't wanted to know Donnie and Nancy. Too different! But we were more alike than different, I knew that now.

24

Then we just sat together in that old Impala. It felt so good to be sitting there and loving horses in that car, with Mrs. Mack!

IT WAS A VERY SUNNY FRIDAY when it happened. I arrived at the stables like always, but something seemed different. I knew that I was getting a new mount. Usually Donnie or Nancy would bring the new horse to me. But today Mrs. Mack went to get it.

As Donnie, Nancy and I waited by the hitching post, I wondered which horse Mrs. Mack was going to bring. Maybe her horse, Apache! When I finally saw the look on Donnie's and Nancy's faces as they looked behind me, I knew it must be Apache. I could hear Mrs. Mack's voice talking softly to the horse.

But when I turned around, I saw it was not Apache. It was my Penny.

I couldn't breathe for a whole minute. Mrs. Mack handed me the reins, her eyes kind of watery-like. I drew up the reins and mounted without a word.

It felt as though time had stopped, the air wasn't moving. It seemed even the birds were watching.

"You made it, Hollywood," Donnie said softly as he smiled.

Nancy nodded and gave a thumbs-up.

I felt my heart connect with Penny's. Her body quivered. She waited for a signal from me to tell her what to do.

I touched her sides with my knees. Penny responded, almost jumping out from under me. I reined her in quickly. My heels were down, my tail tucked under, the reins light in my fingers—I remembered everything I'd been taught. It was second nature now.

"Take her in the corral for a few turns before you head out, Pat," Mrs. Mack called to me. She sat on the fence rails and watched Penny and me intently.

Penny seemed like part of me. She moved as I moved. Her thoughts were mine. We moved like dancers or ice skaters, together. I felt elegant and graceful on her. As I passed each person at the fence, I caught their eyes. Even old Hap was there.

When I pulled up in front of Mrs. Mack, my mouth formed the words "Thank you. Thank you."

Mrs. Mack opened the gate and waved us toward the trail. We trotted through the gate, then we paused. Penny reared and I threw my hand over my head like a cowboy. My heart was singing.

Just then a leaf blew across the road in front of us. A single leaf! Penny stopped so suddenly that she leapt to the left. I lost my balance and fell from her back, hard to the ground.

I held on to the reins, and she dragged me for a few feet. I fought back the tears and the feeling of disappointment, and terror. When Penny finally stopped, I slowly stood up, dazed. My back hurt.

Everyone watched me. I started to lead Penny back to the stables when I heard Mrs. Mack shout, "No, Pat! Get back on that mare. Get on now!"

I couldn't. I was suddenly afraid of Penny. Afraid of her!

"Get back on, Pat," Mrs. Mack coaxed.

My tailbone hurt so much that I could hardly walk, but I knew that Mrs. Mack was right. I had to get back on her. My heart pounding in my ears, I came up beside Penny's neck.

"There, girl," I heard myself saying to her. I gathered up the reins, turned the stirrup, stepped into it, and flung myself back into the saddle. I leaned into Penny's withers. They shivered for a moment. I caught my breath. Then she leaned back into me and I knew she had forgiven my inexperience. She was willing to try again.

I sat straight in the saddle. Penny arched her neck and held her tail high. She reared slightly again, her hooves dancing, and we were under way. My breath caught when she stumbled on the ridge in the middle of the road. But after that her steps were sure and proud.

A touch from my knee and she broke into an elegant trot. Another, and she broke into a rocking canter. I found myself laughing out loud for the sheer pleasure of being on Penny's back.

Everyone around the corral started to clap. Even old Hap. As I cantered by him, I could see a grin. Donnie and Nancy cantered up to me. We exploded down the road together, the three of us!

THERE'S GOT TO BE SOMETHING!

THE AIR SEEMED to be getting a little cooler in the mornings as I arrived at the stable. I knew that I'd have to go back to California for the school year with my Mom soon. I relished the days that were left to Penny and me. We were never apart.

Even the neighborhood kids would call out her name when we trotted by. The smell of burning leaves drifted through the limbs of the trees. I was happier than I had ever been, and sadder at the same time. *Is that possible?*

One day at lunch I burst into tears. No one tried to console me because they all felt the same way. This had been such a glorious summer.

"I am going to miss Penny so much," I finally choked out.

"She'll miss you, too, shugah," Mrs. Mack said as she took my hand.

"I don't want her to be lonely. Who will brush her every day? Who will hug her and tell her how much they love her?" I cried.

"I will, shugah," Mrs. Mack said quietly.

Nancy pointed to a worn photo tacked to the wall: it was of a meadow. "She'll go up north to Ashley to stay on Mrs. Mack's farm with the other horses," Nancy told me.

"Farm?" I questioned. "I didn't know you had a farm," I said to Mrs. Mack.

"Prettiest place you'll ever see," Donnie said.

So the tiny trailer she lived in here wasn't Mrs. Mack's only home! It was at that moment that I realized that Mrs. Mack *chose* to be in Dogpatch with her horses and these kids. Maybe because of the kids!

I looked at her and Donnie and Nancy, and without another word we stood there and hugged each other for the longest time.

Some mornings later, it was overcast and dark when I arrived at the stables. I saw Donnie and Nancy standing waiting for me, and Doc Beck's truck parked in front. Something was wrong. My heart stopped in my chest. I knew it was Penny.

I ran to the back of the lot where her stall was. I found her down.

Doc Beck was leaning over her, holding a mirror next to her nostrils. A trickle of blood was running from her nose.

"Oh, Doc," was all I managed to squeeze out.

He stroked her neck. "A viral infection of some kind, Pat. If we can't get her to her feet, it will most certainly go into pneumonia...."

"Oh, God, please, please," were the only words that came to me. My heart was pounding.

"This isn't good, Pat. When an animal this size lies down with an ailment like this, the lungs will fill with body fluid. She'll drown in her own blood if we can't get her to her feet."

I sank to my knees and pulled her head into my lap.

"Her only hope is for us to somehow suspend her so that she can stand. Right now, she can't support her own weight."

"Then let's try to get her up. We have to!" I screamed.

"She needs a Springer sling," Doc Beck said thoughtfully. "We don't have one at the college." Doc Beck taught there. "We could send to Ann Arbor, but that would take hours. We don't have that kind of time."

"We have to try!" I sobbed.

"I am sorry," Doc Beck said.

"Pat, shugah," Mrs. Mack pleaded.

Penny rattled when she struggled to breathe. Her lungs were already filling. Her eyes looked dim and full of pain.

I watched Doc Beck fill a huge syringe.

"She'll suffer otherwise, Pat," Donnie was saying, through his own tears.

Nancy rocked to her knees. "I'm so sorry, I'm so sorry, Pat."

I started sobbing so hard that drool fell in ribbons from my mouth.

"Mrs. Mack," I said between sobs. "After...will you take her to the farm? Bury her there? Promise me."

34

She squeezed my hand. I knew that she would.

Doc Beck took the needle and held it up to the light to look at the fluid in it, then moved toward Penny. I closed my eyes and held her head next to my heart.

Then the stable door swung open. We looked up. It was Hap.

"Donnie told me," he said gruffly. "Well, you ain't tried everything yet."

"Hap, there's nothing to be done," Doc Beck cautioned him.

"That sling Donnie said you needed… I think we could make it out of this." He pulled a huge canvas bag through the stable door. "It's my riggin', Bernice," he said to Mrs. Mack. "My riggin' from the circus. Got more in the shed if you need it…."

Doc Beck smiled and pulled open the bag. "Hmm, there certainly is apparatus here that we might use, all right."

Everyone sank to their knees and pulled Hap's rigging out onto the floor. I had never seen so many ropes, pullies, brass fittings, and wide pieces of leather in my life.

Mrs. Mack was looking up at a crossbeam above the stall. "This beam will hold her weight," she said.

Mrs. Mack, Doc, and Hap, with us helping, worked as fast as they could to make the sling. "A perfect Springer sling," Doc Beck finally said. Then we managed to ease the rigging around Penny's withers and hindquarters, and we all pulled. But it was no use: we didn't have the strength to get her to her feet.

"Get up, girl. Get up, my beautiful Copper Penny!" I pleaded. But Penny didn't move.

I stopped begging out loud. Instead, I thought as hard as I could. "Please, baby, please!" I said in my heart. Penny's eyes found mine, her ears stood up. She whuffled. "There's my Penny girl baby," I kept saying in my head.

She raised her head. She struggled and rolled, and with each roll everyone pulled on the ropes. Finally, she rolled up onto her front legs, and then with a hearty groan, gave one last push that brought her to both legs. She was weak, but she was up.

WE ALL STAYED with her through the night, loosening the ropes bit by bit as she supported more and more of her own weight.

Doc Beck stayed by her side all night. Her breathing became clearer and clearer. He gave her more shots to help. He kept listening to her chest with a stethoscope. We kept searching his face.

Near morning, he listened again. He snorted and puffed his unlit cigar for a moment. Then he beamed into a broad smile. "She's passed this here crisis," he announced. "This mare is going to be fine, just fine."

Donnie and Nancy cried. Mrs. Mack kept patting their shoulders saying, "We did it, we did it." I noticed old Hap sneaking away like his quiet self. I ran over to him and tugged his hand.

"Thank you, Hap. Thank you," I cried.

He hugged me. Tears ran down his rough old face. Mrs. Mack hugged both of us. The three of us seemed almost like we were one.

As Hap turned to leave, he simply put up one of his hands. He pushed it toward me and with the other hand pointed to the horseshoe-nail ring and smiled.

When that summer ended, I wept the bitterest tears of my life, only to shed tears of pure joy as I went back to the little stable every summer for the next seven years. Dogpatch and the folks who were at the stable on the night of crisis were changed after that summer.

Old Hap was a new man. In time, he took a wife, the widow who lived across the street. He became known as a helpful, almost jolly neighbor there in Dogpatch. Donnie had his dream, too, to be a veterinarian like Doc Beck. He went to veterinary school right there in Lansing. No one really knows who helped him, but we have a good idea.

Donnie returned to Dogpatch long enough to marry Nancy, then they moved down to Shelbyville, Tennessee.

Mrs. Mack gave Penny to me to have for my very own that next summer, and I kept Penny at my dad's until I was eighteen and went away to college. Then Dad returned Penny to Mrs. Mack and her farm in Ashley, Michigan.

In the summer of my twenty-sixth year, I visited Mrs. Mack on that little farm with my two small children. She led us to the meadow where Penny stood. Penny turned and looked at me and whuffled. She walked slowly toward me. Her muzzle was flecked with gray, but her eyes were still full of grace and intelligence, her neck still arched and her tail held high. My eyes followed her contours once again. She was still perfect.

She stood there while the sun danced through the leaves of the overhanging trees, her coat gleaming like a bright copper penny.

In the winter of my thirtieth year, my father called to tell me that my sweet copper Penny had died. "Patricia, she was almost twenty-eight years old! What a horse, what a horse," he said over and over. " Mrs. Mack told me to tell you that she kept her promise."

I knew that she would.